Breaking the Cycle to Low Self Esteem

Breaking the Cycle to Low Self Esteem

A KINGDOM APPROACH TO WOMEN IN POVERTY IN THE 21ST CENTURY

§

S. Sabrina St. Clair

Copyright S. Sabrina St. Clair, 2009

All Rights Reserved

ISBN-13: 9781537014746
ISBN-10: 1537014749
Library of Congress Control Number: 2016913284
CreateSpace Independent Publishing Platform
North Charleston, South Carolina

Contents

Abstract

POVERTY IS FOUND FOREMOST IN the most marginalized group of people. This project is concerned with one such group—the single African American mother. Low self-esteem is a trait that is associated with many of these women. I posit that there is a correlation between low self-esteem and poverty. Left alone, this cycle, supported by societal systems, becomes a generational problem conveyed from mother to daughter. This project creates a collaborative relationship between the community and the church to help the participants break the cycle of low self-esteem by helping them to understand their self-worth. The goal is to help liberate these mothers and daughters from the oppression of humanity's injustice so that they may see themselves as the precious human being that God created them to be: fearfully and wonderfully made.

Acknowledgements

§

I GIVE HONOR AND GREAT thanks to God who has remained faithful to me throughout the task. For "...He who began a good work in [me], will complete it..." (Philippians 1:6 KJV)

Rhema Christian Ministry for trusting in the vision and purpose that God has given to me; and walking with me as we do ministry together.

Hal Bennett, Felecia Cook, Diane Mosby, Michelle Thomas who labored tirelessly with me throughout the process, offering me their wisdom, expertise, listening ear and time.

Rev. Dr. Michele Jacques-Early who would not settle for anything less than the best from me.

Participants who trusted me to process my project on them

Loisann's Hope House

Washington regional area of the Boys and Girls Club of Fredericksburg

My mother, Jacquelyn LaForest, who encouraged me to continue

Daughters Quiana Chareese and Shauna Chania who shared me with the project and showed me a more excellent way.

Dean Kinney and Dr. Victoria Pratt who believed in me when the process first began in 2001.

STVU faculty and staff who challenged me to grow outside of the familiar box of ministry

Hughey St.Clair – the Love of my life, my friend, confidante, husband and partner in ministry who has made sacrifices and loved me enough to let me be the woman I was purposed to be.

My Ancestors who were called, but never got the opportunity to be chosen, on whom shoulders I stand.

Introduction

§

Breaking the Cycle of Low Self Esteem and Poverty: A
Kingdom Approach to Women in Poverty in the 21st Century

FOR TWENTY-FIVE YEARS, A CERTAIN Woman was tagged with a name given from birth that she felt spoke negatively to who she was. Finally, when she became an adult, she changed her name. However, the negative effects of her given name and how she viewed it left her with a low self –esteem that not even a name change was able to readily correct. The affects of being born with dark skin and kinky hair in the 1930's, while all of her other sisters were pecan tan had taken its toll on her. So low was her self-esteem that she dared not venture out into her career choices. Many sat and listened to this Certain Woman as she talked about how close she had come to being a dental assistant; almost being able to enter into the military; and finally, how she missed an opportunity to travel as back-up singer to a famous gospel artist. Her value of herself led her to instead follow the dreams of a man whom she married, was divorced from and then became a single mom with three children. The lack of additional training and fear of venturing into a career caused the Certain Woman to succumb to what appeared to be a lifestyle of poverty.

Her low self-value did not end with her. Although she tried to encourage her children, there was an element of her fears that resided with them. She shielded them from those who were able to help them to go further and dream dreams bigger than their existence. She blocked opportunities for their future growth by denying them the right to after school activities and become involved with social organizations. She loved them, she shielded them and she refused to let them venture beyond their social/economic standards. This world that she knew was a safe world for her and she wanted to keep her children in the same safe environment she had come to know. The youngest daughter decided at the age of 18 that enough was enough, and one day moved out on her own. But the cycle of low esteem was not broken. Neither was the cycle of poverty broken. While this young lady was now on her own and working full time in an office as a clerk, she had become a part of the working poor. This cycle continued until she found herself married, divorced, a single mom and remarried again. The more she became in touch with her inner qualities, the more value she began to give to herself. The cycle was beginning to break. After the birth of her daughters she returned to the church, got in touch with her spirituality, and surrendered herself and her children unto God.

Biblical teaching, positive affirmation, and the opportunity to explore their talents and desires were some of the ways she was able to help her daughters develop a positive self-esteem. She was able to instill in them an appreciation of who they were—beautiful, intellectual, gifted girls created by God. Self-value began to increase in both the mother and her daughters with the collaboration of the church and the community. Through biblical teachings, charm schools and volunteering with social agencies, her children began to develop. The cycle broke, and now her daughters have good self-value, are following the career choices they selected, and are definitely not poverty stricken.

As we dare to enter into this conversation, it is my hope that some woman or some girl will understand God's love for them and live the life of liberty and prosperity that God intended for them. Those who are captured in the cycle of low self-esteem are those who have found themselves lost in a world far beneath their purpose and yielding to elements that prevent them from being all they are called to be. It is my theory that there is a direct correlation between low self-esteem and poverty.

WHERE DO WE BEGIN?

Researches reporting in the *Journal of Consumer Research* assert that a constant lack of needed life provisions can lead a person to develop low self-value. Being deficient in these necessities of life has the potential to lead persons to develop an unhealthy respect for material gain. Therefore, "by the time children reach early adolescence, and experience a decline in self-esteem, the stage is set for the use of material possessions as a coping strategy for feelings of low self-worth."[1] This cycle of low self-esteem and materialism then becomes so entwined that one behavior will foster the other. Many African American single mothers find themselves caught in this vicious non-ending cycle of low self-esteem and material gain. They devalue themselves because they are not able to supply the necessities of life for their family, and yet they are unable to provide the necessities they need because the value they have for themselves will not enable them to go out and position or market themselves fairly in society.

Low self-esteem can cause one to respond by lowering their expectations of success and accepting failure as the norm. Little effort is put into new ventures because they doubt they can be successful. Finding that comfort zone because they are afraid to try anything too new will limit their potential for growth. This feeling can cause them to become overly dependent and allow others to make life decisions for them. There is a constant putting down of self that consumes any assertiveness they may have possessed. Low self-esteem can cause the person to feel like a failure to everyone and to themselves, thus causing the person to remain trapped in a womb of self despair. Unfortunately, many times this cycle continues from one generation to another. Many mothers who are struggling with self-esteem have mothers who also had to deal with the same emotional turmoil.

---

1 Lan Nguyen Chaplin and Deborah Roedder John, "Growing Up in a Material World: Age Differences in Materialism in Children and Adolescents," Journal of Consumer Research (December 2007), 480-493

It is the purpose of this book to help women to come out side of the womb of despair and break the cycle of low self-esteem. Once they come to see themselves as God sees them, I believe that they will begin to enact the principles that will help them to expect and seek financial gain. In order to accomplish this task, the church and the community must work together. I hope this information will enlighten the Church and the community and provide additional insight and tools to help women in their midst to rise and fulfill their destiny.

CHAPTER 1

Stages of Change

THE PARTICIPANT'S ROLE

ANY CHANGES IN SELF-ESTEEM MUST begin first internally. To do this, all entities involved must rely on the principles of the One who created us and called us good. It is imperative that the person seeks the wisdom of the Creator and declares as David, "...I am fearfully and wonderfully made..."(Psalms 139:14 NKJJ)

It is also true that with all faith, there is a level of action God expects of us that is required to bring about the reality. This is where the community comes in. I believe that the community has opportunities available that coexist with the training of the church, and together life can be changed. The woman's voice is silenced because there is little value that either the church and/or the community apply to her self-worth. Both organisms find themselves talking at her and seldom listening to her. Her self-esteem is under attack, but unless someone is attentive to the situation, it goes unnoticed. Plans are often times implemented to give a hand-out to solve the immediate need, but not enough plans are going forth to help eradicate the problem at the root. The church and the community organizations are often times in combat with one another to fulfill their quotas, but lack the sensitivity of the holistic need of the individual. The community wants to do what they do without the church. The church wants to do what they do without the community. The persons who get left out are the single unmarried women who feel neglected and unworthy. This was evidenced to me at a community gathering.

As I sat in the midst of a room of social action agents summoned at the command of the city official I listened intently at the concerns that were presented to us. Critical social issues, including education, teen pregnancy, drugs and violence in the community were being addressed across the room. What I felt to be most alarming was the heads of all of the social agencies of the community gathering did not reflect the same culture of the persons they were intending to reach. As I continued to observe, I noticed that the church community was not invited into the conversation. How can one address the concerns of the community and not include the church community? How can one address the concerns of the community without including representation of the community? Then I asked; why was I not invited? I pastor a church in the midst of the community they were talking about! I just happened to stumble into the event without a formal invitation. I guess you can say I was a meeting crasher.

For too long the church has found herself separated from the mainstream conversations focusing on social justice. Many of the persons that are targeted for the numbers in the social agencies are either members from the community we are called to serve or representatives from our own congregations. The number one target people for the programs are young single women who are having children. Ironically, this is the same population that we find in our churches. Many of the women that the agencies are servicing come dressed up on Sundays perpetuating a lifestyle that is not reflective of their true existence. The extent of their wealth is many times placed upon the backs of their children and on themselves. This brings forth a disguise to mask the real lack that exists in their lives. The cry for help will go forth, but not to the open ears o the church. Instead the community service organizations will hear this cry and will be called to answer it. Now I believe that in reality the church is aware of the situations in which the women find themselves, but is reluctant to respond for fear of being held accountable. Everyone sees the woman as a statistic that is in need, and will cost money to fix. Many programs have been established to provide fish for the woman, but not enough is being done to teach her how to fish. I believe that the impoverished woman is hiding behind a low self-esteem that does not permit her to be more than society has labeled her. In the church she is encouraged to continue to pray for help, but not enough time is invested in helping her to come to an understanding of who she really is in Christ Jesus. This is evident in the lack of training that is administered to the woman who finds herself feeling low. The church and the social community agencies share the responsibility of serving as change agents in the lives of these underprivileged mothers and daughters. The mother must also be willing to assume a participant's role for the process to be effective.

Church Role

The Bible is very much concerned about the problems that are associated with the poor. There are many references to the poor and the obligations that the church has to address these needs. Poverty has a disproportionate place in society. Based on previous and current research, there appears to be a correlation between low self-esteem and poverty that exist in many mothers and daughters, especially in inner cities.

The Church may benefit from taking on this effort as a ministry and not as a project reliant on government funding because the project must have the freedom to use biblical principles. If a system is built based entirely on government funding, then the church will face the possibility of operating at the whim of the same system that in the past has not consistently invited the African American single mother to the table. It is my premise that there are a disproportionate number of mothers caught in a cycle of low self-esteem who are living in poverty in urban areas. Many of these women are victims of low self-esteem that is generational. Low self esteem exists for many reasons: knowledge, exposure, and systemic oppression. In order for the cycle of poverty to be broken, the church, the community and the workplace must collaborate in addressing the self esteem issues that are prevalent among many mothers and daughters who are poverty stricken.

I believe that in order to minister effectively to persons that are demeaned, we must first have compassion for them. My ministry is an advocacy for the mothers who feel that they are trapped in a world of poverty and forced to deal with the negativities associated with it. I have empathy for them because I was once one of those women. I was the little girl in the inner city streets of Baltimore reading my way out of my circumstances. When I see the mother and the daughter I see myself. When I look into their lives, I see the anger and frustration that they are feeling as they try to make a living out of meager wages. Yet, their anger does not scare me. I too was angry. I am still angry. I am angry, but I have learned how to use my anger effectively. I am angry at a system that thrives at the expense of those whose voices have been silenced. I am thankful for the gift of anger. It is this anger that never lets me be comfortable with just me and mine. It is this anger that will cause the church to assume the role of participants in helping to break the cycle of low self-esteem and poverty among this vulnerable population. One thing that I do know is Jesus came to set the captives free. According to John 8:36 (NKJV), "Therefore if the Son makes you free, you shall be free indeed."

GOVERNMENT'S ROLE

The government has a role in ensuring social justice for the marginalized group. Accordingly, Dr. Schutt says,

There are powerful religious fundamentalists all over the world and in various cultures that seek to define for women in categorical and absolutist terms what their own good is and to constrain women to act accordingly. These fundamentalisms also define the meaning of nation and family in categorical terms, promoting self-sacrifice and often war, while impeding those who are influenced by these ideologies from acting on their own desires for personal fulfillment and happiness. Some government and private institutions, moreover, derive enormous material benefits from women's cheap labor and from women's traditional family care giving roles. There are forces in society that benefit from women ending up in prostitution, remaining illiterate, or being confined to economic and social conditions, which, from girlhood on, subject them to recurrent violence and abuse.[2]

Twenty-five years ago the state of Illinois, recognizing the correlation between poverty and low self-esteem, developed their own version of welfare to work. Their intentions were to help persons on welfare to overcome low self-esteem created by years of being considered the lowest part of society and effectively content with others in the job

---

2 Ofelia Schutte, *Cultural-Cultural Communication and Feminist Theory in North-South Contexts."* Ed Naomi Zack (Malden: Blackwell Publishers, Inc. 2000)45-64

market.[3] Edward T Duffy, director of the Illinois Department of Public Aid cited little sense of worth as one of the characteristics of the people in their programs. Duffy affirmed, "You can give people some education and skills. You can even find a job for them. But if they don't have confidence in themselves, they probably won't make it."[4] The author identified the goal of building the belief in aid recipients that they can, indeed, compete in the work place and are responsible for finding and keeping jobs as a vital component of the program.[5] Another member of the staff attributes many of the fears and anxieties that inner city women experience in seeking employment to the lack of role models to offer skills.[6] This was the plight of Odessa Triplett, a thirty-two year old woman in the program who had never held a job. For Ms. Triplett the cycle of poverty that existed between mother and daughter were evident in her life. Her mother was also a victim of poverty and low self-esteem and had never had a job. Ms. Triplett dropped out of school at age 14 and became pregnant at age 16. She has two children, and neither of the fathers contributes support.[7]

Through such reports our government realizes the necessity for the increase in self-esteem to alleviate poverty in the inner city. However, the funding that was placed in such programs has been greatly depleted. Today we recognize that while the funding for such projects has diminished, problems for women have not. Instead, low self-esteem continues to disproportionately foster poverty amongst single women mothers in our inner city neighborhoods. This discrimination that the female experiences maintains inequalities, lessens economic security, and exposes women to undeserved disrespect. The devaluing of the woman causes her to have a low appraisal of herself, and encourages

---

3 Dirk Johnson, *Anti-Poverty Program Seeks to Build Self-Esteem*, (Special to the New York Times, February 21, 1988.), section 1 page 24 of the New York edition.

4 Ibid.

5 Ibid.

6 Ibid.

7 Ibid.

low self-esteem. I posit that through a positive model, young girls will identify with who they are based on God's plan. What humanity determines as her flaw, God may call perfection.

In the past decade the number of women living in poverty has increased disproportionately to the number of men. "The rate of poverty is even higher in African American single-parent families, in which two out of every three children are poor."[8] African American women head the majority of these impoverished single-parent families.[9]

---

8 SingleParentMatch.com (Powered by Successful Match) 2001 — 2009.
9 Ibid.

CHAPTER 2

Psychological Framework
for Women in Poverty

§

Low self-esteem is systemic and stems from internally and externally induced sources. In Carol Gilligan's book entitled *"In A Different Voice"*[10] she discusses theories of various psychologists that are relevant to girls and women. Gilligan shows how many psychologists do not account for the different experiences of women. Instead they emphasize autonomy, individual rights and separation as necessary components to successfully develop. According to Freud's Oedipus' theory, girls' sexual development is inadequate at the time of adolescence and they are psychologically wounded. Freud associates male puberty with the onset of libido and he sees puberty as a period of repression for women. He suggests that puberty for women raises self-awareness of her inferiority and her acceptance of "the fact of her castration."[11] Nancy Chodorow[12], a feminist sociologist and psychoanalyst, challenges Freud's contention that women are developmental failures. She acknowledges the social structure for girls as being different from boys, but Chodorow attributes this social structure to the bonding of mother daughter/relationships. Girls are an extension of their mothers and inherit the same nurturing skills; whereas boys experience a separation from their mothers that prepare them for more life challenges and self-identity. This separation helps boys to spend more time looking for and establishing themselves. Chodorow's theory is more in line with Gilligan's theory that male gender identity is threatened by intimacy because masculinity is defined through separation while femininity is threated by separation because femininity is defined through attachment.

Dr. Janet Lever,[13] Professor of Sociology who specializes in gender studies continues the theory that learned behavior helps to form the self-identity of girls and boys. She concludes that the games boys and girls play as children are instrumental in their roles as adults. According to Lever the sports that boys participate in give them a social advantage over

---

10 Gilligan, Carol, *In A Different Voice*
11 Ibid. 436
12 Ibid. 432
13 Ibid. 9-11

women. Through sports they develop interpersonal skills that strengthen their ability to deal with competition, whereas girls' social activities are more confined and intimate. Gilligan shares Lever's position, which says boys learn to play with their enemies and to compete with their friends by participating in controlled and socially approved competitive situations. However, girls' games are more restrictive and intimate fostering greater empathy and sensitivity. I would assume that Lever equate sports such as football and basketball to boys and social activities e.g. glee clubs and drama classes for girls. While there is some validity to what Lever says, I would suggest these thoughts of Lever's could be disputed when we assess the rise of girls participation in competitive sports e.g. basketball, gymnastics and soccer in the 21st century.

Gilligan and Lever both believe the interpersonal skills developed by men from their youth prepare them with a confidence needed for authority, while women are said to assume human resource positions that are relational and nurturing. Economically, the relational and more human resource types of jobs like social worker and teacher tend to pay less than the technical jobs that are assumed by men. Gilligan concludes that women's development is tied to their relationship with others and they feel a strong sense of responsibility to the world.

Catherine Collins[14] is a health educator who is an advocate for African American women health issues. She shares my beliefs in that many inner city African American women are exposed to social negatives associated with poverty, i.e. crime, drug use, incarceration, unemployment. The detriment of these negative characteristics result in lowered self-esteem as the women are left trying to define their personal value to themselves and to their children in the midst of less than adequate housing and the basic necessities of life. Scholars have determined that dark skin tones on low-income women have negative effects on self-esteem and self-efficiency.[15]

---

14 Maxine S. Thompson, "The Blacker the Berry: Gender, Skin Tone, Self Esteem and Self Efficacy," *Gender & Society*, Vol. 15, No. 3, 3356-357(2001)DOI:10.1177/08912243010 150032c2001Socioogist for Women in Society.
15 Ibid.

Poverty is oftentimes associated with dejection that generates low self-esteem causing the African American women to deal with the psycho-social stresses of being of a darker skin tone and being female in a white male driven society. In many areas, the female population continues to be the greatest victims of the persistent poverty in our communities. They continue to be overlooked in the midst of the pains of financial deficiency.

Another relevant study relating psychological and physiological conditions was conducted in the *Annals of Behavior Medicine, which* showed 40% of women reported clinically significant depression and 43.3% were below the poverty line. Dr. Mary deGroot shows how the physical conditions impact the psychological conditions of women. "Multivariate logistic regression analyses indicated that non work status, lack of home ownership, low appraisal of one's economic situation, low self-esteem and increased life events was significantly associated with depression at baseline."[16] She concludes from her study, that economic and social factors in the lives of poor African American women need to be addressed. Research conducted by Timothy J. Haney suggests "blighted and decaying urban neighborhoods are read as disinvestments by both residents and city governments, and therefore, these images are internalized and incorporated into resident's psychological makeup."[17]

---

16 Mary deGroot. Annals of Behavioral Medicine (2003, Vol. 25. No. 3,) p. 172-81

17 Timothy Haney. "Broken Windows and Self-Esteem: Subjective Understanding of Neighborhood Poverty and Disorder" *Paper presented at the annual meeting of the American Sociological Association, Montreal Convention Center, Montreal, Quebec, Canada,* August 10, 2006 *Online* <PDF>. 2008-06-11 <http://www.allacademic.com/meta/p94664_index.html>

CHAPTER 3

The Issue of Esteem

LOW SELF-ESTEEM HAS BLOCKED MANY women's potential to venture beyond the invisible boundaries that they have established. Is it possible that the establishing of the invisible boundaries began in the sanctity of the home? Linda Hollies in *Inner Healings for Broken Vessels* connects the low self-esteem of women to their families. It is in the families that young girls look to their fathers for affirmation and to their family members for acceptance. When there is no father present, or where family members are not accepting of the young girl there is a possibility she will develop into an adult who is in constant pursuit of affirmation from others. Many of the women we will address are women who have themselves bound by self-inflicted invisible boundaries because they were not affirmed by those close to them who could have made a difference in their lives. Often times this lack of proper guidance will cause the woman and her daughter to not believe in themselves enough to see beyond their current circumstances. These women's lives become dysfunctional because they are psychologically trapped in the boundaries established by persons who benefit from her lack of self-esteem. Understanding the possibility of this dysfunction helps us to recognize the need for intervention at young ages to help our girls deal with the issues they encounter.

Pamela Brubaker completed a study to help address the theory that women's issues have not been fully appreciated. This study discovered a number of revealing strategies about women in the world.

Women account for 70 percent of the world's people who live in absolute poverty. Women work two-thirds of the world's working hours, produce half of the world's food, and yet earn only 10% of the world's income and own less than 1% of the world's property. Worldwide, a quarter of all women are raped during their lifetime. Depending on the country, 25 to 75 percent of women are regularly beaten at home. Between 10% and 50% of women report they have been physically abused by an intimate partner in their lifetime. Over 120 million women have undergone female genital mutilation. Women hold only 12% of parliamentary seats worldwide. Women account for 2/3rd's of the world's illiterate adults, and girls account for 2/3rd's of the world's children without access to education."[18]

Financial, political and social issues for women have not been taken seriously enough to constitute a change. Until women are entered into the dialogue, change is not to be expected.

For the Black woman, tactics to deal with the many dilemmas she has faced have been both conventional and unconventional. Dr. belle hooks highlights one example as to how this is operative in the lives of Black women. She suggests that black women have had to rely on lying just to survive. This strategy has been both essential and detrimental for the growth and development of women's self-esteem and earning potential. Lying has historically been used to make life bearable in a repressive environment and to help one survive because "skillful lies could protect one's safety."[19] However, in attempting to be successful in assimilation, we have fostered an outer appearance that does not line up with our current state of affairs. Appearance becomes very important to the black community as an image is sought to be maintained. This is a lie that does not protect, but causes the person to escape reality. Hooks identifies this condition as a problem. She exposes the wickedness of classism. "The privileged classes have convinced the poor and underclass that they must hide and deny the realities of their lives while the privileged go public, in therapy, sharing all that they might have repressed out of shame, in order to try and heal their wounds"[20] This behavior prevents the person from rising to their full potential. Because a stigma of shame is placed on poverty, the poor will tend to cover up their problems and live a façade life. I believe in order to effectively break the cycle of low self-esteem; we have to help the women

---

18 Brubaker, Pamela K. *Women Don't Count. The Challenges of Women's Poverty to Christian Ethics* (Atlanta: Scholars Press 1994) 24

19 Hooks, belle. Sisters of the Yam and Self-Recovery. (Boston: South End Press, 1993), 12

20 Ibid.

get beyond the lie. The lie participates in them being mislabeled. The lie supports the whole economic statement. Personal struggle is connected to the systemic reality. belle hooks challenges women to stop allowing what others think about us to determine our reality. Instead we have to decolonize our minds, and understand and appreciate our own experience so that we can counter the dominant stereotypes.

Women do not share the same moral norm of human dignity that men do, either in the religious traditions or secular, according to Brubaker. This devaluing fosters economic injustice. When society belittles the worth of a woman, it contributes to lowering the self-esteem of this woman. The lowering of her self-esteem, or self-value, makes her a prime candidate for poverty.

Likewise, Linda Hollies says that women must face the reality that they often have to push pass the unrealistic expectations society has placed on them.[21] To gain control we must grapple with our inner pain, emotionally express our hurt, and look at alternative actions.

Nell Painter gives us an example through the life of Sojourner Truth. For Sojourner Truth freedom was released for her twenty years before she actually saw the physical manifestation of it. Although she was a slave, Sojourner Truth realized that her situation would not always keep her in captivity; her mind was free before she was physically free.

WORK, SELF-ESTEEM AND SELF-EFFICACY AMONG AFRICAN AMERICAN WOMEN

Sojourner Truth recognized that economic empowerment was a call to freedom that begins in the mind. Economic empowerment was not the mode that one could expect from a former slave. When Truth was faced with the need to pay for her debt, Neil Painter declares that Mrs. Truth

---

21 Linda Hollies, *Inner Healings for Broken Vessels: Seven Steps to a Woman's Way of Healing*, (Upper Room Books, Nashville, TN. 1992) 45

looked around at the work that was being done by others like Frederick Douglas, emulated his success, and achieved her goals.

Maxine S. Thompson shares this view. According to her recent article, "low income shapes self-esteem because it provides fewer opportunities for rewarding experiences or affirming relationships. In addition there are more negative attitudes associated with behaviors of individuals from less privileged socioeconomic stats than those of a more prestigious one."[22]

The data listed below is a portion of the research that established the relationship between self-esteem and work. It is well documented in the sociological social psychology literature that work experience impacts self-evaluation.[23]

The two dimensions of self-evaluation discussed in the literature are self-esteem and self-efficacy. Self-esteem refers to an individual's sense of self-worth, whereas self-efficacy indicates a sense of control or competence.[24] The study investigating the relationship between work and self-esteem shows that work conditions or job characteristics are positively related to self-esteem. The work condition that most studies in this area find to be most consequential for self-esteem is work autonomy. Findings from several studies reveal that the degree of freedom or control the worker has over his or her work has an impact on self-esteem.[25] The jobs most available to untrained persons in poverty do not offer workers much freedom or control.

---

22 Maxine S. Thompson and Verna M. Keith, "*The Blacker the Berry: Gender, skin tone, self--esteem and self-efficacy,*" *Gender & Society*, Vol. 15, No. 3, 336-357 (2001) DOI 10.1177/089124301015003002 @ 2001 Sociologists for Women in Society)318

23 Ibid.

24 Rosenberg, 1979; Gecas, 1982; Schwalbe, 1985.

25 Mortimer and Lorence, 1979; Staples et al., 1984.

CHAPTER 4

Breaking the Cycle

MENTORSHIP

OUR MOTHERS AND DAUGHTERS TODAY are in need of persons they can emulate and who will help them to achieve their goals. Therefore, mentorship is one tool to use to help women and girls develop a healthier self-esteem and become all that they are destined to become. The article entitled *Power, Poverty and Urban Policy* helps to identify the necessity for mentoring to change a person's perspective of themselves and their situations. Sanford Kravitz, the author, says the "Charity Organization Societies saw the answers to poverty in retraining the indigent, improving his moral standards, removing from the influences of depraved family life, and showing him to the knowledge and counseling of an experienced worker or skilled upon class volunteer.[26]

Conversely while Kravitz encourages unity, the article entitled: *Living in Isolation: Women's experiences of poverty and exclusion*, revealed how social isolation has increased among impoverished women. *Living in Isolation* was the result of the research that was generated from *Report Card* written by Colleen Reid and Pamela Ponic. [27] The theoretic framework for this research conducted was psychological, developmental as well as feminist. Reid and Ponic contend that poverty has been a vehicle to keep women socially disengaged. According to their study, the exclusion resulted in isolation, loss of identity and a sense of powerlessness. When they do not engage in the necessary social relationships, girls are not introduced to the necessary skills to help them when encountering various groups of people. This can impact their self-esteem to cause them to settle for the familiar ways of life they are accustomed to. The intimidation can diminish the reality of obtaining a college education, or seeking a career versus a job.

---

26 Warner Bloombert Jr., and Henry J. Schmandt, "Power, Poverty and Urban Policy." Volume 2. (*Sage Publications Inc.*, Beverly Hills, CA 1968) 259

27 Report Card, October 15, 2004 Living in isolation: Women's experiences of poverty and exclusion By Colleen Reid & Pamela Ponic

However, Kathryn Tanner declares "In the same way one could cultivate crops or animals in order to better them, one could cultivate one's person, specifically one's highest capacities of faculties, in order to develop or perfect oneself."[28] Based on her statements in *Theories of Culture*, the quest for liberation could be realized if a person's personal perception was cultivated through mentorship, or self-awareness trainings. That seems easy enough, yet we are still faced today with a culture of African American women and girls who are still struggling with low self-esteem and poverty.

Helen Black conducted research with a population of fifty women who were in poverty, but their self-esteem was not low.[29] Black showed how the women used prayer as a consolation for their lack of economic substance. They had accepted their hardship as a divine plan and expected to be rewarded in the next life. I will look deeper into this area to see if we actually use God as an escape for complacency. I will also be looking to see if fear that was not addressed in childhood, simply became substituted with a mirage of excuses, with the church being the catalyst.

The Church

Dr. Boydkin Sanders decrees that the African religious community in America has been led away from its "historic role as protector and guardian of Justice for African and other oppressed people in America."[30] This abandonment leaves many people coping with the injustice of economic impoverishment. Sanders suggests that classist practices have emerged within our African American communities and those who find themselves on the prosperous side of this struggle are content and can no

---

28 Tanner, Kathryn, Theories of Culture, Fortress Press, MN. 1997.p.4

29 Poverty and Prayer: Spiritual Narratives of Elderly African-American Women Journal article by Helen K. Black; Review of Religious Research, Vol. 40, No. 4, 1999.

30 Boykin, Sanders, "Blowing the Trumpet in Open Court," New Jersey: African World Press, Inc., NJ 2002), 167.

longer identify the voices of the terrorists.[31] The terrorists as identified by Sanders are the oppressed.

Dr. Edward Wimberly's pastoral perspective on the victims of those who suffer economic injustice is in alignment with Dr. Sanders. Wimberly says that his years of pastoring, traveling and studying suggest that society has deemed these people as outcast. In his book entitled *Relational Refugees*, Dr. Edward P. Wimberly speaks to people who have found themselves as outcasts in society. He defines refugees as those who are alienated because they do not fit in or belongs to mainstream society. The impoverished African American Woman would certainly qualify for this title. She is an economic refugee. I define economic refugee as the financially lacking, destitute and disadvantaged person who does not fit the classical norm for gainful employment.

Concurring with this theory, Dr. Harris let us know in *Black liberation* that the Black preacher's responsibility is to fill the void of the lost voice. As a liberation theologian, Dr. Harris says that preaching ought to be trans-forming. "The process of transformation begins with a new understanding of consciousness which requires a mental and spiritual transformation."[32] According to Kathryn Tanner this is where cultures develop. Through the transformation of the mind, we can develop a culture that will not be afraid to be liberated. If liberation is a precondition of transformation as Harris shares, then we must conclude that transformation is the external display of an internal release. In other words, before the African American woman can actualize change physiologically, she needs to be psychologi-cally set free do so. This freedom should be preached from the pulpits.

Dr. Musa Dube declares this liberating preachment must come from a person who is able to justly confront, expose and arrest the imperialis-tic strategies of the bible. This is because economic and political hege-mony was behind the formation of the interpretation of the Bible, and it is still the governing formation of our society. I suggest that whenever economics and politics are an issue, we also find the issue of injustice of

---

31 Ibid.

32 James H. Harris, Preaching Liberation, (Fortress Resources for Preaching, 1995) 9

women. The victimization of women of color has caused these women to either embrace the Bible interpretations wholeheartedly, or disregard it in all of its contents.

Dr. Painter suggests that one of the reasons the plantation slaves were able to survive psychologically was they employed a system of evangelical religious beliefs that denied the master's religious and social ideology of white supremacy and black inferiority. The plantation slaves were brought from a culture that worshipped the Spirit of God, and their culture saw God beyond the bible. As a matter of fact, many did not own a bible in their own country. Their awareness of God was far superior to their conditions. This is the God that we must introduce to the inner city women and girls of color who are greater than they think they are.

As the voice of the single mothers living in poverty cry out to the church, I hear the voice of the Lord still hailing from Matthew 11:28 declaring, *"Come unto Me all you that labor and are heavy laden and I will give you rest."*[33] Many single mothers are laboring hard, yet yielding substandard benefits. They are overloaded and burdened with the conditions of poverty. Here Jesus is extending a personal invitation to those who are working hard to make a difference, yet are weighed down with the unyielding challenges of life. This invitation extends beyond the isms that plague our society.

I believe that the Jesus that Matthew 11 talks about is the Jesus that cares about the holistic well being of all that are weary and tired. This includes not only the middle to upper class young professionals that are consuming the attention of many churches today; but it is an invitation to underprivileged mothers as well. The community of faith consists of them all.

The church is the community, yet many times we are alienated from the tangible problems that the community encounters. While the church focuses on the spiritual needs within the four walls of the brick

---

33 The word rest is *anapauo* and it describes a cessation from toil. James Strong, *The Exhaustive Concordance of the Bible*, (Hendrickson Publishers, MA 1984) 373.

and mortar, the parishioners leave a haven of peace to go to their personal sanctuaries of hell. We are challenged to help those who voices have been silenced by their social/economic status to the point that they have given up out of desperation. We are challenged to begin by helping the most marginalized persons in our community who need to be introduced to Jesus—the one who will truly give rest. For us, this person is the indigent African American single woman and her progeny who is seeking to break the cycle.

God has given the church this essential mission. It is the responsibility of the church to raise the conscientization of the effects low self-esteem has on the quality of life for women and girls. When the church accepts this assignment, we will see mothers and their daughters begin to realize their self-worth and rise from their destitute positions.

Through the writings of these authors, we experience a glimpse of the challenges the African American women and girls face today. First we see that African American single mothers face the greatest challenges economically. Secondly, we see that girls are directly impacted by the behavior of their mothers. And thirdly, low self esteem impacts psychologically as well as physiologically. Through the support of our Black academic, spiritual and faithful intellectuals who walk in integrity, I believe we can make a difference in our culture. I believe that if we seek God's direction we can together break the cycle of low self-esteem and develop a successful plan to destroy the yoke of poverty for African American women who are disproportionately poor.

BIBLICAL PERSPECTIVE

God is very much concerned about the problems that are associated with the poor. There are many references in the Bible regarding the poor and the obligations that the church has to address their needs. Although the poor many times lack the proper attention of the church, they are never out of the watchful eyes of God. There are two keys that are vital in concept, Psalm 139 and Numbers 26.

In Psalm 139:14, the Psalmist declares, "I will praise You O Lord, for I am fearfully and wonderfully made. Marvelous are Your works that my soul knows right well."[34] It is this revelation that we want the mothers and daughters to embrace. In this pericopy an elderly David recognizes God as omniscient and omnipresence, not as dry doctrine, but in the context of personal relationship. God knows and cares for David because God made David. All human life belongs to God who has the power over life and death. No one can escape God's presence and nothing is hidden from Him. Yet from intimidating David, this truth leads him to wonder, praise and prayer.

Having lived through both times of adversity and times of privilege, David as an elder man can honestly look back from the time of his youth to his present state and reflect on his experience. It was through his trials and accomplishments that he was able to develop a personal relationship with God. David saw himself as God saw him. He was fearfully—Hebrew meaning is to revere or to cause fear[35]-- and wonderfully made. David recognizes the love that God has for him. David says that God's works are marvelous. Marvelous in Hebrew indicates to distinguish, put a difference or set apart.[36] This understanding gives David the freedom to be who he is and accept that he does not have to measure up to anyone's standards or acceptance but God. In this pericopy the readers are invited to this intimate conversation that David is having with his Lord. David recognizes that no matter what happens, God is in ultimate control. This level of control is not to be relinquished into the hands of people, for people will let you down or control you according to their own personal agendas. David realizes that the relationship that he shares with God is not to be taken for granted, but it is to be cherished.

This Psalm offers to the mothers and daughters an opportunity to also reflect on God and God's attributes. Psalm 139:4 invites the mother into a conversation that qualifies her based on the standards of God. The mother

---

34 Strong, James; Exhaustive Concordance of the Bible; Hendrickson Publishers, 1984.

35 Strong, James; Exhaustive Concordance of the Bible; Hendrickson Publishers, 1984.

36 Ibid.

and daughter may not understand their uniqueness in God, but like David, they are invited to appreciate it in spite of the poverty that they may find themselves existing in.

Historically, too often inner city single mothers have been the greatest victims of persistent poverty and the church has been silent bystanders or contributors. Unfortunately, being a silent bystander and/or perpetrator against the economic empowerment of women has not been an unusual stance for the people of God. In the 27th chapter of the book of Numbers when God had Moses distribute wealth amongst the people, we find five unwed women, the daughters of Zelophehad, who were being overlooked in the distribution of economic empowerment simply because of their gender. "…The daughters of Zelophehad…stood before Moses, before Eleazar the priest, and before the leaders and all the congregation, by the doorway of the tabernacle of meeting, saying: "Our father died in the wilderness; but he was not in the company of those who gathered against the LORD, in company with Korah, but he died in his own sin; and he had no sons. Why should the name of our father be removed from among his family because he had no son? Give us a possession among our father's brothers.'" (Numbers 27:1-4 NKJV) Other children of God who knew that the absence of land for the daughters would surely lead to their demise surrounded the women. Land in the Old Testament represented an identity and a means of being self-supportive; inheritance of it was relegated to men only. With the death of their father and having no brothers who could inherit the land and provide them a life of prosperity, Zelophehad's unwed daughters knew destitution was inevitable. Instead of accepting the fate they were facing, they decided to challenge the rules of the system. Their non-conforming behavior was indicative of the self-value they held. They believed they were worthy enough to be counted into the inheritance even if it meant going against the multitude.

Zelophehad's daughters exemplified tenacity, tact, courage, wisdom and grace to stand up for what they believed. Had it not been for their high self-esteem the daughters of Zelophehad would have found themselves in a dependent state of existence. While the Biblical text does not reference the mothers of the daughters, I believe that from a young age, someone instilled in them their self-worth. Since the mothers spent more time with the daughters than the fathers, I believe that the mother had great influence on their self-value. The daughters of Zelophehad were faced with many obstacles. The culture of their day did not esteem women to be any more than child bearers, and property. Female self-worth was dependent upon the value society would place upon them. Their societal status was the lowest on the human scale, next to the female daughter.

This is the same place that many African American women today find themselves. Their self-worth is based upon whom they are attached to. Those who have the boldness that Zelophehad's daughters had and dare to speak above their circumstances are the ones who are able to walk into the inheritance that God has promised to them. Unfortunately, life circumstances have greatly diminished the self-esteem of many single mothers. The challenges of proving or even realizing your self-worth are not an easy task when you are immolating a mother who was psychologically bound by the elements of low self-esteem herself.

Before Zelophehad's daughters confronted Moses they went through the channel of commands set before them. According to the custom of their era the women would first approach their tribal leader. Moses would have been at least two to three steps into their search for help. The rejection that they must have been experiencing at each level did not cause them to give up. The esteem they held for themselves was high enough to cause the women to be persistent until they got their desired results. When Moses was confronted by the women regarding their dilemma Moses went to God. God responded, "The daughters of Zelophehad are right...you shall indeed let them possess an inheritance among their father's brother..." (Nu. 27:7) unfortunately, the level of high esteem that the daughters of Zelophehad garnered for their fulfilled promise is not operational in the lives of all women. There are many unmarried women ensnared in a life of low self-esteem who are not fulfilling their potential.

One reason that we sometimes lack the courage to believe in our potential is due to lack of self-confidence. Self-confidence is not to be confused with arrogance. Arrogance is a haughtiness or egotism that generates from self-importance. On the other hand, self-confidence is a self-assurance that God has imparted a part of God's self inside of us that is good in the eyes of God. In Psalm 139:14 David portrays self-confidence as he declares, "I will praise thee O'Lord, for I am fearfully and wonderfully made. Marvelous are Your works that my soul knows right well. For some this may seem like a Scripture of arrogance, but David was expressing gratitude to God for doing for him only what God could do.

To understand this, we must go back to the thirteen verses preceding. Throughout the text David recognizes that God knows him intimately. David spends the first 13 verses recapturing the intimacy of their relationship. David declares that God knows him physically, mentally and spiritually. There is no part of David's life that is not known by God. In these stanzas, David speaks of God being omniscient (1-6), omnipresent (7-12) and omnipotent (13-18).

Those in desire of building their self-esteem must also come to the same conclusion; as God's creations, custom made by the efficient, powerful, creative, loving hands of the one and only true and living God. To love ourselves, is to love what God has done. To acknowledge that we have it going on is truly to acknowledge that God who has made us divinely orchestrated us and made no mistakes.

YOUTH PERSPECTIVE

Low self-esteem affects the daughters of the mothers as well when the cycle is not broken. For there to be a change in the self-esteem of the daughter, the elements of her life must not mirror those of her mother. Unfortunately low self-esteem is not readily identified in young girls because their behavioral changes are often erroneously diagnosed as hormonal. Jane Mosely, of the Center for Demography and Ecology wrote in her report on "Poverty, Welfare and the Self-Esteem of Adolescence":

I would argue that self-esteem is important in its own right as well as a mediating variable for other child outcomes. In an ideal world we should care just as much about a child's emotional state as the level of education they achieve. Additionally, this sense of worth would seemingly affect other child outcomes. If a child feels he/she is at a loss to affect life circumstances, or feels worthless, these feelings will likely affect many of his/her accomplishments. And indeed, Wilson and Portes[37] found that self-esteem was related to both educational attainment and success in the work force.[38]

Moreover, in the *Journal of Abnormal Child Psychology*, researchers established that low self-esteem and hopelessness in children were related to socioeconomic disadvantage.[39] The authors structured their argument saying that girls' socioeconomic disadvantage predicted lower levels of self-esteem based on a study conducted by Levy. When poverty is not alleviated in the field of a child, it can extend into the life of the adult.

In addition, scientific evidence has been established to show fear as one of the prominent emotions of children in poverty. *The Effects of Poverty on Teaching and Learning* helps to give good scientific reasoning to the behavior of children in poverty.[40] Without an understanding of the psychological makeup of these children, they are mislabeled and misplaced in the educational system causing them greater difficulties in their development. "Poor children often have a feeling of helplessness, low self-esteem and may be fatigued. Thus when their brains downshift they will not go any further than addressing survival skills."[41] This

---

37 K. L. Wilson, and A. Portes, A. "The educational attainment process: Results from a national sample." *American Journal of Sociology*, *(1975)* 81:343-363

38 Jane Mosely, "Poverty, Welfare and Self Esteem of Adolescence," www.ssc.wisc.edu/cde/nsfhwp/nf.h69.pd, Accesssed January, 2008.

39 Rob McGee, Shelia Williams and Shyamala Nada-Rraja, "Low Self-Esteem and Hopelessness in Childhood and Suicidal Ideation in Early Adulthood." *Journal of Abnormal Child Psychology*, (August, 2001)

40 http://www.teach-nology.com/tutorials/teaching/poverty/9/June 16, 2008

41 Ibid.

research offers a complete tutorial to help teachers teach the children and create an environment that will cause learning to be effective. The references used by the author are extensive, bringing many dynamics to the study. The basic components of this study reflect the various environments, the emotional needs, scientific evidence, many references to aid, and possible solutions. Creating a model of entrepreneurship and service is one way that we create an environment that encourages the children to learn, without the restrictions that they associate with the traditional classroom. It is our desire to help the children rise outside of their internal box of helplessness to recognizing their internal strengths and God given talents.

WOMANIST PERSPECTIVE

Katie Canon, Jacquelyn Grant, Stacey Floyd Thomas and Emilie Townes are just a few of the womanist theologians who have helped the single impoverished African American mother reclaim her voice in the social/economic marketplace. "Womanist," Thomas declares, "are concerned with how theoretical insights and identity politics concerning the life and work of Black women work to facilitate liberationist scholarship and anti-oppressive social praxis."[42]

Dr. Katie Canon shares that slavery was a mechanism used to strip Black women of their humanity and declared them to be 'brood sow and work ox.'[43] She was forced to imitate whatever the role she was cast in at the moment. Angela Davis is in agreement with this callous mishandling of women, as she states, "...When it was profitable to exploit them as if they were men, they were regarded, in effect, as genderless, but when they could be exploited, punished and repressed in ways suited only for women, they were locked into their exclusively female roles."[44]

---

42 Stacey M. Floyd-Thomas, *Shades of Purple, Womanism in Religion and Society*, (New York: New York University Press, 2006) 6.

43 Katie G. Canon, *Black Womanist Ethics*, (Georgia: Scholars Press, 1988) 31

44 Angela Y. Davis, *Women, Race & Class* (New York: Random House, 1981) 6

The oppressive race casts the southern bell as the idealized depiction of a perfect woman. Using the southern belle as the epitome of beauty, White America created the mammy stereotype of a Black woman as a counterpart to the southern belle. The mammy was created to further denigrate Black women. Emilie Townes contends that the fictional "mammy demonstrated the benefits of maintaining the color line and how Black women behaved under proper white control." Mammy became a property that was owned by White America and assigned to the new Black woman as her identity. Townes states, to treat identity, as property is one form of the cultural production of evil.[45] Aunt Jemima became the mythological epitome of White America's conception of the Black woman. She was an image that they owned and the created image was personified as a desexualized being whose purpose for existence was to be a maid or a servant to the White woman and her family. This further impoverished the Black woman and according to Jackie Grant, impoverished Black woman in a racist society are considered facsimiles of womanhood and considered to be less than human.[46]

As the Black woman was stripped of her culture and her inner and outer beauty so was her self-worth diminished. The years of degradation yielded many Black women with identity crises that sent her looking for redemption. She had to be defined and society dictated that the White woman would be the measuring gauge. Anything beneath the standards was considered to be substandard. Many African American women fought through the pretext to establish their own identity and self-worth. They fought for the right to be considered equal. They dared to push through the doors of opportunity. However, for as many as were able to escape, there were as many left behind with their minds flawed by the residue of slavery and racism. Captured by hopelessness, many inner city single African American mothers were snared in the traps of poverty with little hope for escape. African American men as well as women are challenged

---

45 Emilie M. Townes, *Womanist Ethics and the Cultural Production of Evil*, (New York: Palgrave Macmillan, 2006) 39

46 Jackie Grant, "Poverty Womanist Theology, Ministry," editor Paul Plenge Parker, *Standing with the Poor*, (The Pilgrim Press, Cleveland 1992) 55

with the affects of poverty. However there are distinctions of women's poverty that differ from men's poverty. Diana Pearce in 1978 coined the term of 'feminization of poverty.'[47]

With her self-esteem diminished by society, the Black woman found herself oppressed. Not only was she left to challenge her own spirituality, or self-worth as a child of God, but she had to deal with the destruction of her dignity that comes with oppression. She experiences what Grant declares to be a loss of human dignity. Grant theorizes that oppression "reduces human beings to objects, violates their own personhood, makes a mockery of peace and justice, an is a sin that contradicts the righteousness of God the dignity of all humanity."[48] Our young girls are fragile, and if not shown a different way, they may fall prey to the devices that have captured their mothers and a cycle of low self-esteem. In the 20th century, oppression of the African American single mother was a reality that left she and her children victimized by a system of injustice in the world and in the church.

In the 21st century, many African American mothers with no husbands are still facing oppression and many of the people of God remain silent bystanders or contributors. Dr. belle hooks defines oppression as the lack of choices.[49] Choices, like oppression, create differences in social status and quality of life. Women who are deemed to have low self-esteem are more likely to lack the right choices necessary to help them reach their full life potential. Low self-esteem affects the daughters of the mothers as well.

According to Dr. Katie Cannon, upon the time of entering into the world the African American woman and the African American girl are the lowest in social status with only the African American boy being in the middle of the two. While there are many who have climbed outside of the stereotypical boundaries set for them, there are still a number of young Black women and children who have found themselves trapped in the system. Society has ignored, put down, and misunderstood this marginalized

---

47 Ibid.52

48 Ibid.57

49 belle hooks, *Feminist Theory from Margin to Center*, (Boston: South End, 1984) 5

group. The maltreatment that impoverished women face is not triggered by social justice systems only.

Womanist theologians have been prudent in raising the awareness of the historicity of African American women and the challenges that have endured. These same women have also offered us a better way based on their intellectual insight and years of research. This constitutes a theological mandate. Jackie Grant says we must strive to restore the basic dignity of all creation. Three challenges she presents to the Christian Community are that Christians must:

- Relinquish their theologies of domination by which some maintain control of the women, the poor and the stranger.
- Relinquish their theologies of charity where the poor are given enough to lessen the guilt of the middle class but not enough to strengthen themselves for the long fight against the culture of poverty.
- Relinquish theologies of domination and submission that uphold a white father God who dominates non-whites and non-males, thus ensuring both the racialization and the feminization of poverty.[50]

Maya Angelou never failed to amaze me. She was able to pin words that speak volumes and cause one to halt. She declares, "There is no agony like bearing an untold story inside of you."[51] Maya's words are inspiring as many women are carrying promises and purpose in their wombs in search of a midwife who will help them deliver their potential. Hidden in the crevices of their souls are the untold stories that have prevented many impoverished women from living a fulfilled kingdom life. The impact of these untold stories have caused many women to have a lower self-esteem and less than insignificant reflection on their personal worth of themselves that extends into the wombs of their daughters' self maturation as

---

50 Jackie Grant, "Poverty, Womanist Theology, Ministry," editor Paul Plenge Parker, *Standing with the Poor*, (The Pilgrim Press, Cleveland 1992) 56-58

51 Maya Angelou Quotes, Self Help Daily Inspirations http://www.selfhelpdaily.com/SelfHelpQuotes/MayaAngelouQuotes.html/accessed June 2008.

well. I define a woman with low self-esteem as a woman who has been devalued and sees herself as inferior to others.

There are many young girls and their mothers who have toiled over their purpose in life and their self-worth that have not had the opportunity to reflect on their personal worth. We have embraced slogans, e.g. 'too blessed to be stressed,' while all the time hurting inside. They are seeking an undetermined value of their sense of worth and their cultural milieu has become their measuring gauge. I believe there is another message out side of society's definition of their cultural milieu that has been distorted. I believe that the message of love Jesus left behind has been distorted. Jesus not only represents the love from the cross as a demonstration of God's love for us; but the sacrifice and forgiveness in search of the victory won on the cross for them. Carol Saussey says that Jesus' message is essentially a challenge. Choose life - which is to love and be true to yourself and your neighbor and through that love and fidelity, to love and be true to your God. According to Saussey divine punishment is a label for painful experiences that people endure. Their story may not be our story, but their pain ought to be felt to cause one to act or reconcile. Many females are discounted because of their symptomatic behavior, without any consideration for why the behavior exists. It is only after we have empathy and not apathy for their weakness that others can genuinely be used to be effective change agents in their lives.

One example is noted in Rev. Dr. Renita Weems's book entitled *Listening for God*. At the time that she entered into the arenas of Black female scholasticism, ministry, professor and writer the existence of other women occupying these positions were not as prevalent as it is today. (And even now, the representation is disproportionate.) Weems says "I worked so hard for so long to prove that I had what it took to make it in the predominantly male professions I had chosen, enduring the long lonely nights of study..."[52] Life had placed upon Weems the need to be accepted at whatever cost, even the cost of her marriage. Before becoming a mother, she could not relate to the

---

52 Renita J. Weems, *Listening for God: A Minister's Journey Through Silence and Doubt*, (Touchstone, New York, N.Y. 1999) 140

Scripture "and when the Lord saw that Leah was hated, the Lord opened her womb." (Genesis 29:31) Weems was troubled over the value that was placed on the woman's ability to bear children and it's inference to God.

In order to be able to have any compassion for Leah, Weems found that she first had to identify with Leah. Having struggled with her own level of self-value Weems ascertains, "I wanted to believe that it was possible both to engage in fulfilling work as a ministry, scholar and writer and to find satisfaction in the daily obligations of mothering. But at the moment I felt like Leah, too drained of energy and time to figure out how quickly blessings can turn into burdens."[53] Weems relief came when she was able to get in touch with her inner self and carefully assess each of the areas of her life that impacted her being. And so it is with many under-privileged mothers who are burdened and angry. They too must get in touch with the source of their anger, even if it begins with them.

They are angry at a system, at society and at themselves. Unfortunately, when their anger meets the silent anger of the person who is able to administer help they often find the ordeal tumultuous. Could it be that the persons that they were seeking help from did not want to be reminded of their situation because they were once in their shoes? Saussy decrees "If persons can deal effectively with their own anger, they will overcome their fear or intimidation in the presence of another angry person, unless the other is a violent person."[54] I believe that to contend with the anger in someone's life, we must first acknowledge the anger within our selves. Anger is not an emotion that has been readily accepted into the Christian community. Yet, it is this anger that should cause the African American Church to rise up and engender effectual change in the lives of disadvantaged mothers and daughters. Without the church's intervention to recognize this need in impoverished women, this anger has the potential to go inward and ignite a cycle of low self-esteem.

Stemming as far back from the era of slavery the Black woman has experienced degradation because of her personal appearance. With all of the ways that the women has been negatively defined by society and culture,

---

53 Ibid. 140
54 Carol Saussey, The Gift of Anger, (Westminster John Knox Press: Louisville, KY) 113

there have been those who were able to overlook the labels and defy the status that their culture and society has placed on them. Transformative social-justice begins with understanding ones identity.

HOPE AND RENEWAL

This leads me to my final example of hope and renewal—the church. Heidi Neumark declares, "Advent is when the church can no longer contain its unbearable unfulfilled desire and the cry of anhelo bursts forth: Maranatha! Come Lord Jesus! O Come Emmanuel."[55] She shares how the church she ministered in used the right curriculum to help the members learn about the Lord and embrace the social justice they deserved and Christ was demonstrated. Hope and renewal is experienced when we take on the challenges of teaching various cultures how to love, respect and help one another. We must have the audacity to hope- "Help Other People Effectively"[56] Effective Christian Education is critical in the church if our members are to grow from milk to meat. It is the churches' responsibility to help its congregation to live out the life that God has intended for each and every person. Correct teaching is imperative. The author declares: "Where is the outrage in our churches? Where are the tears?"[57] I surmise the tears are shedding and the impoverished mothers and daughters in our churches and communities who suffer at the hands of the oppressors experience outrage. I also conclude that the biblical text is crying out in outrage. Crying out for the church to embrace the biblical text and allow its empowering principles of compassion, call to action, love, and collaboration to manifest.

These are the tools the Certain Woman is now using to help her to evolve into who she is destined to be. It is never too late. The cycle can be broken.

---

55 Heidi Neumark, *Breathing Space, a Spiritual Journey in the Bronx*, (Boston: Beacon Press 2003) 211

56 S. Sabrina St.Clair, "Essay: Reflections on Hope," (October 15, 2009) 2

57 Heidi Neumark, *Breathing Space, a Spiritual Journey in the Bronx*, (Boston: Beacon Press 2003) 208

www.ingramcontent.com/pod-product-compliance
Lightning Source LLC
Chambersburg PA
CBHW060649290526
45793CB00001B/459